SCIENCE MYSTERIES

WHERE DOES THE SUN GO AT NIGHT?

AN EARTH SCIENCE MYSTERY

BY **AMY S. HANSEN**
ILLUSTRATED BY **KOREY SCOTT**

CONSULTANT:
JON AHLQUIST, PhD
DEPARTMENT OF EARTH, OCEAN, AND ATMOSPHERIC SCIENCE
FLORIDA STATE UNIVERSITY
TALLAHASSEE, FLORIDA

CAPSTONE PRESS
a capstone imprint

First Graphics are published by Capstone Press,
1710 Roe Crest Drive, North Mankato, Minnesota 56003.
www.capstonepub.com

Books published by Capstone Press are manufactured with paper
containing at least 10 percent post-consumer waste.

Library of Congress Cataloging-in-Publication Data
Hansen, Amy.
  Where does the sun go at night? : an earth science mystery / by Amy S. Hansen ;
illustrated by Korey Scott.
    p. cm.—(First graphics. Science mysteries)
  Summary: "In graphic novel format, text and illustrations explain how Earth's
movement causes day, night, and changes in the seasons"—Provided by publisher.
  Includes bibliographical references and index.
  ISBN 978-1-4296-6098-3 (library binding)
  ISBN 978-1-4296-7176-7 (paperback)
  1. Earth—Rotation—Comic books, strips, etc.—Juvenile literature. 2. Seasons—
Comic books, strips, etc.—Juvenile literature. 3. Graphic novels. I. Scott, Korey, ill.
II. Title. III. Series.
  QB633.H365 2012
  525'.35—dc22   2011001016

EDITOR: CHRISTOPHER L. HARBO
DESIGNER: LORI BYE
ART DIRECTOR: NATHAN GASSMAN
PRODUCTION SPECIALIST: ERIC MANSKE

Printed in the United States of America in Stevens Point, Wisconsin.
072013   007586R

TABLE of CONTENTS

Why Does the Sun Move Across the Sky?

In the morning, the sun rises. At noon, it hangs high above you. In the evening, the sun sets.

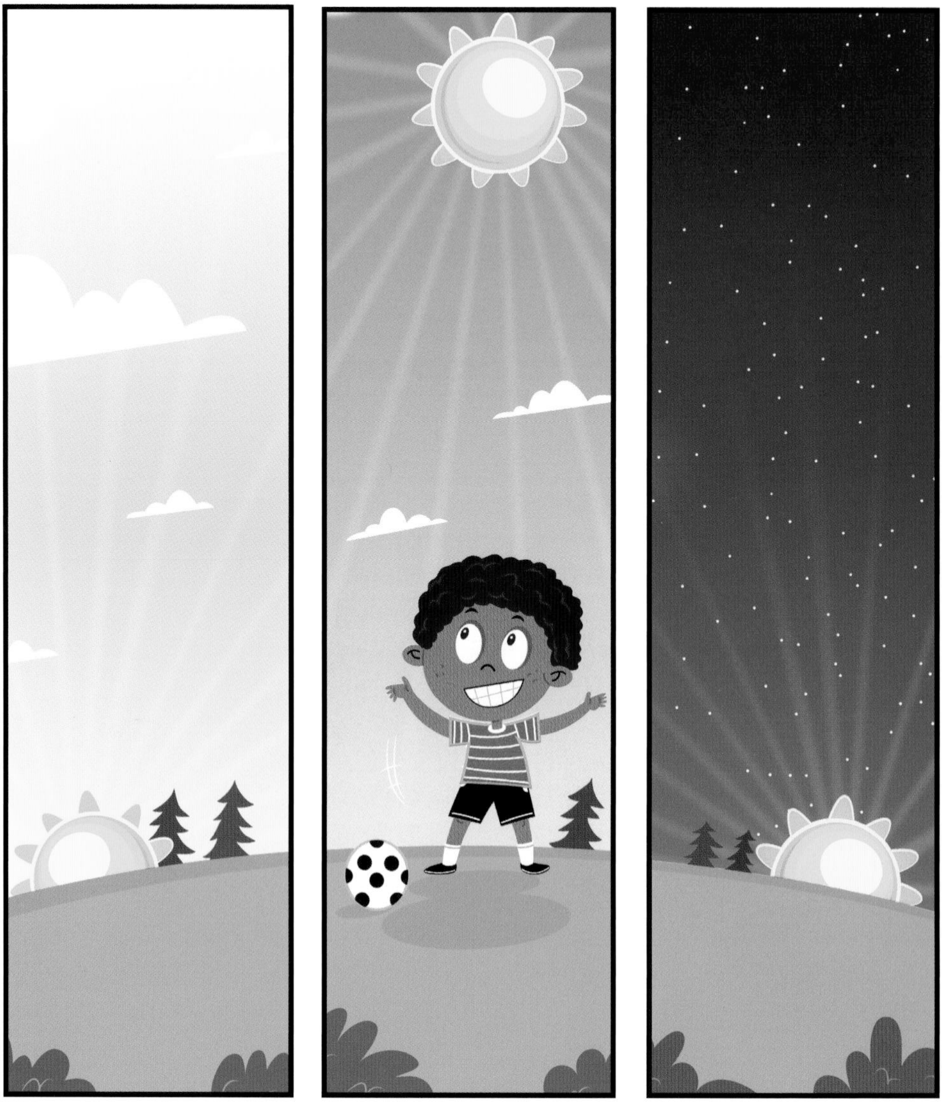

Every day, the sun seems to move across the sky. And every night, it disappears.

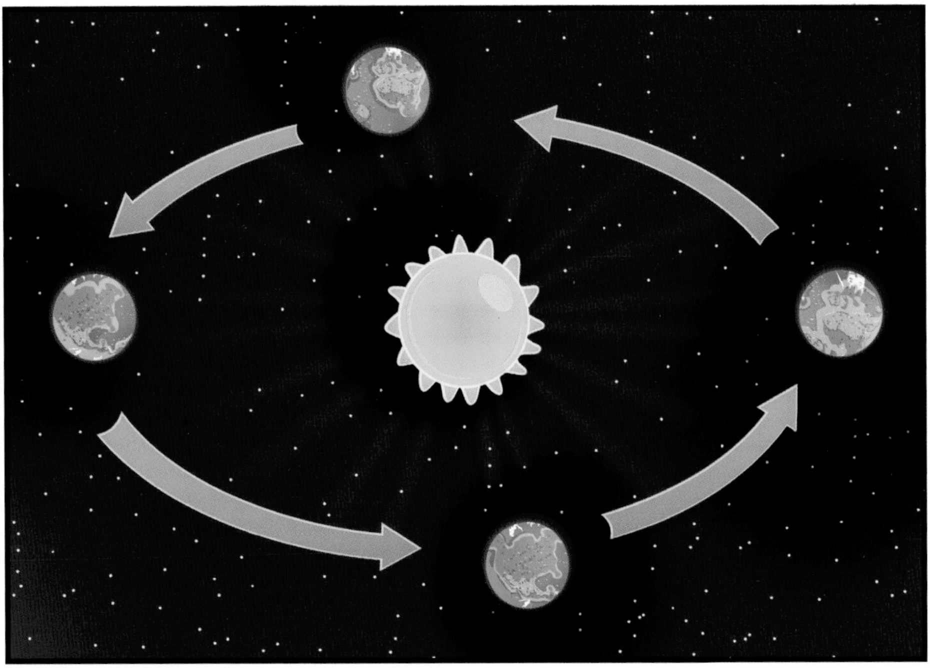

But the sun isn't moving at all. Earth moves as it circles the sun.

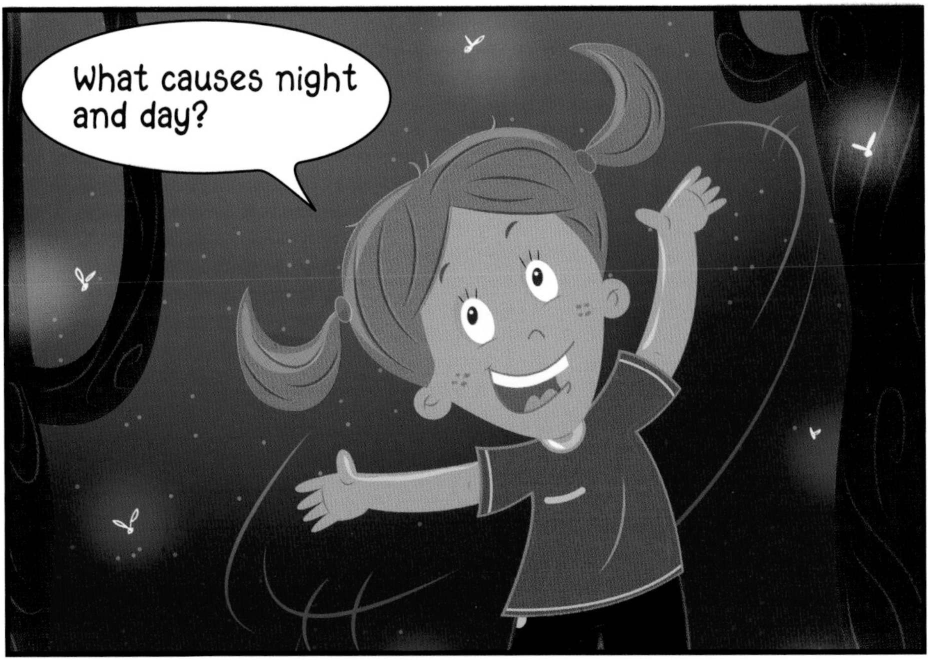
What causes night and day?

Earth spins like a giant merry-go-round.
Its spin causes day and night.

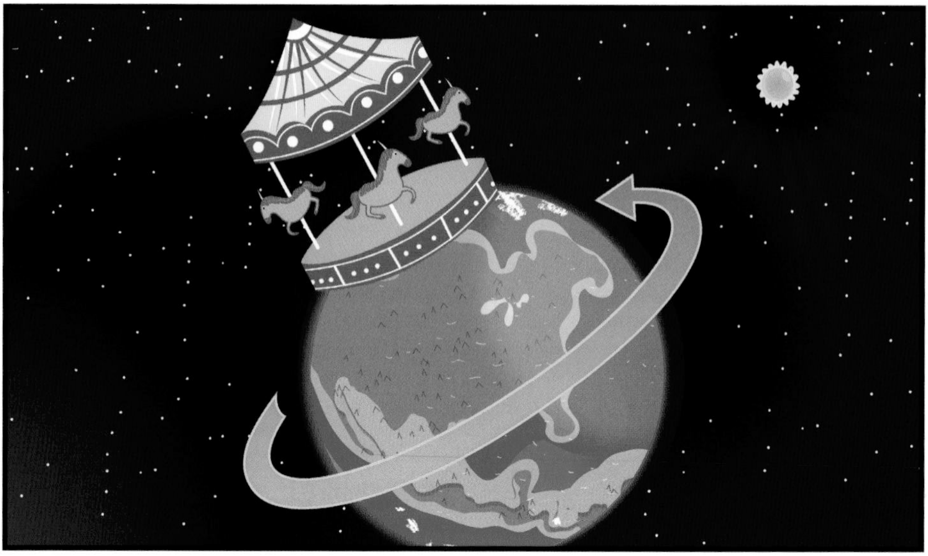

As Earth spins, sunlight hits one side.
Shadow covers the other side.

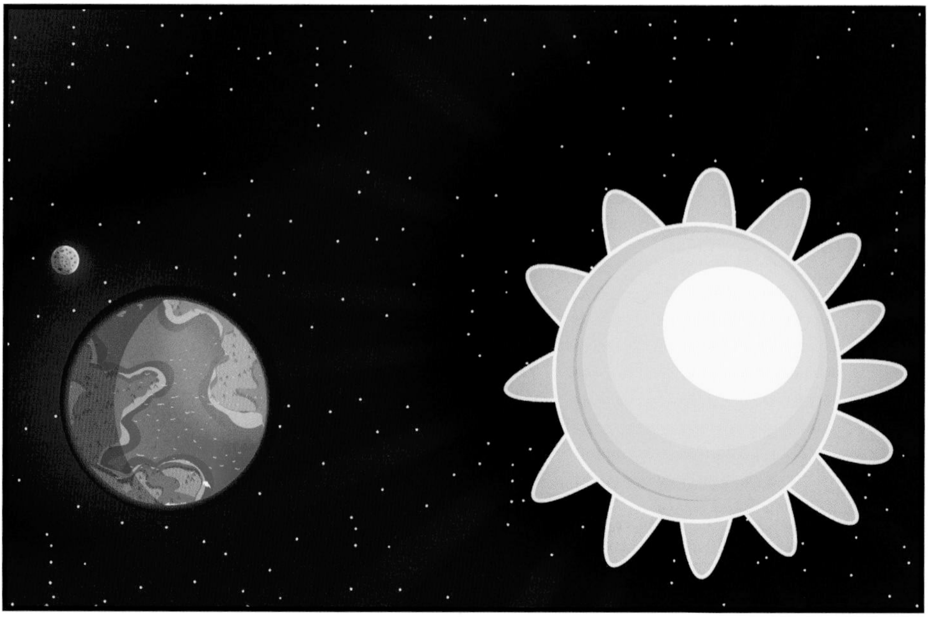

Daytime happens when your side of Earth faces the sun.

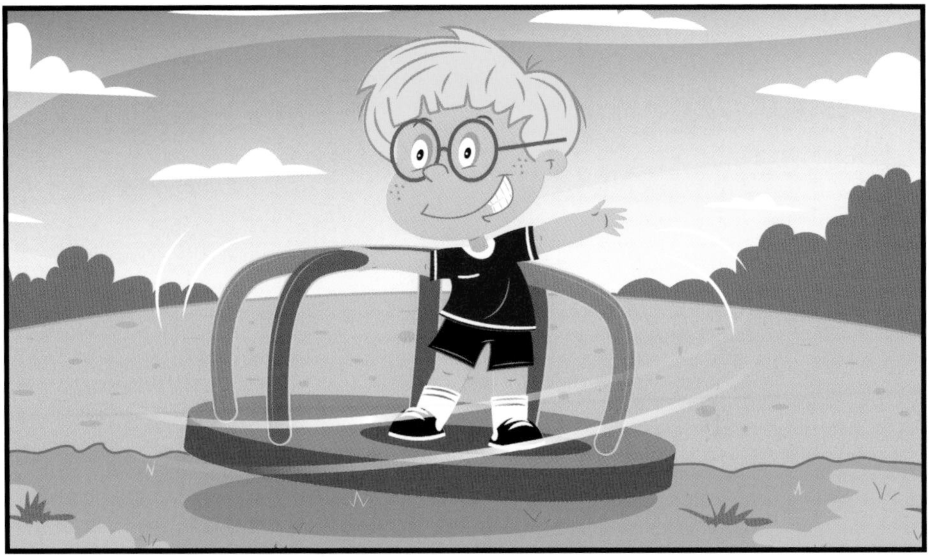

Nighttime happens when your side of Earth turns away from the sun.

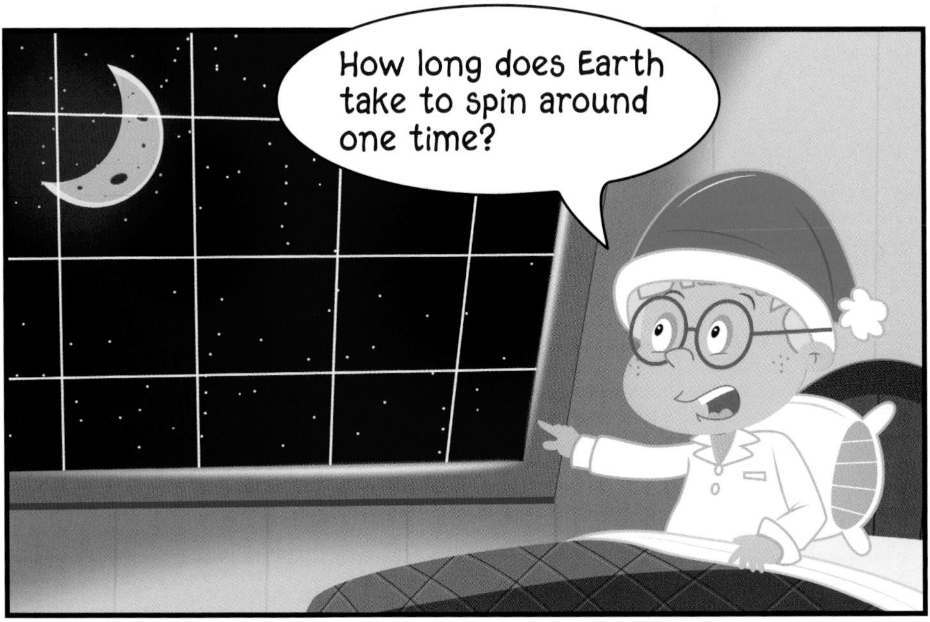
How long does Earth take to spin around one time?

Earth spins around one time in 24 hours. Each day begins at midnight when it is dark outside.

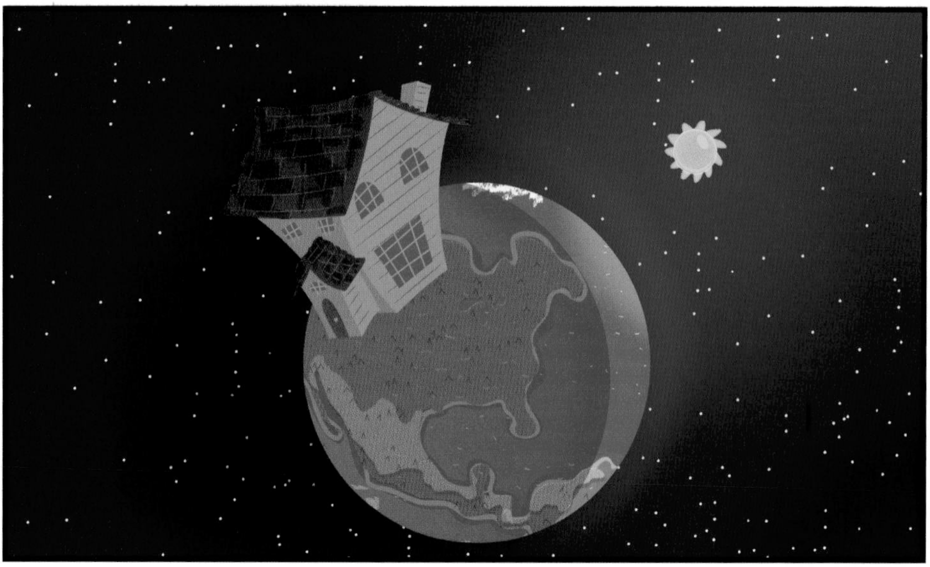

By dawn, your side turns enough to get a little sunlight.

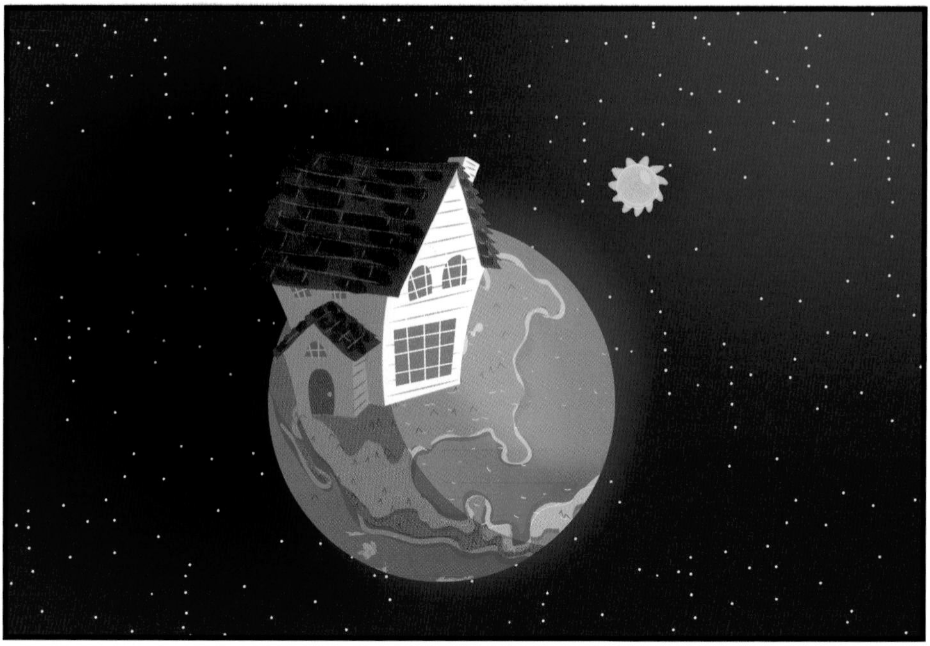

At noon, your side faces the sun most directly.

By dusk, your side turns away from the sun.

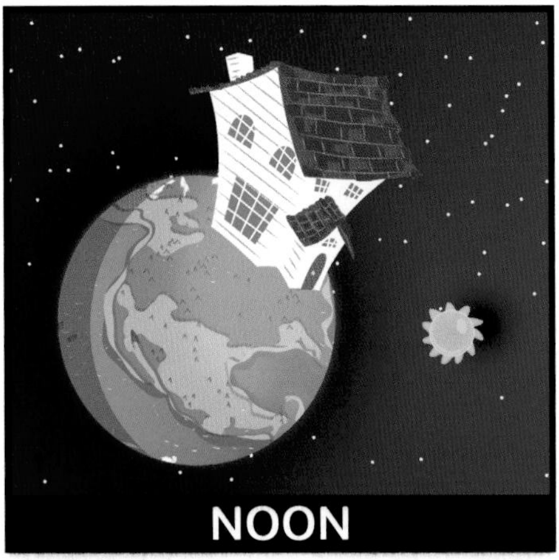
NOON

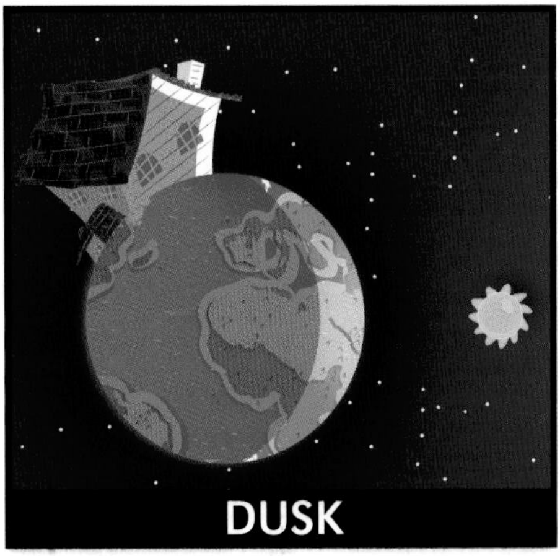
DUSK

The day ends at midnight. Then the next day starts.

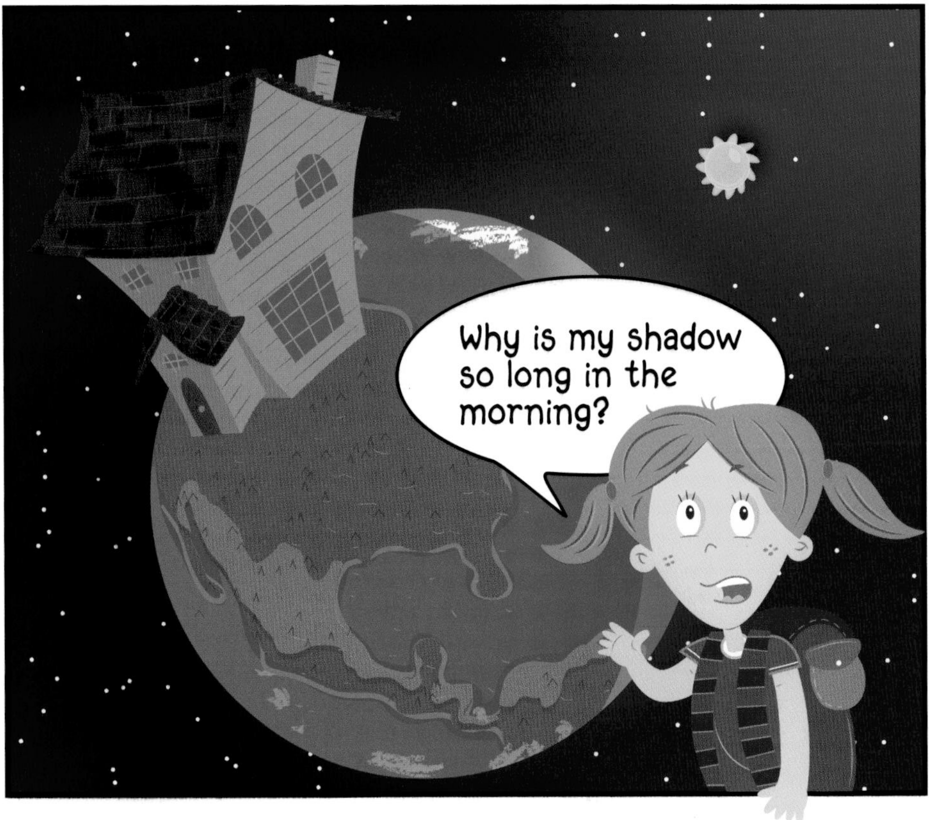
Why is my shadow so long in the morning?

Why Does My Shadow Change?

The sun's place in the sky makes shadows long or short.

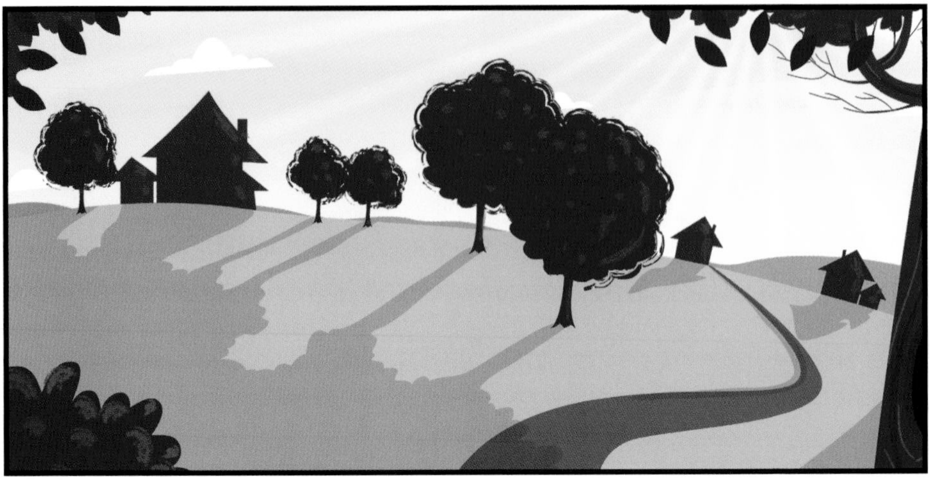

In the morning, the sun hangs low in the sky. Sunlight hits your body from the side.

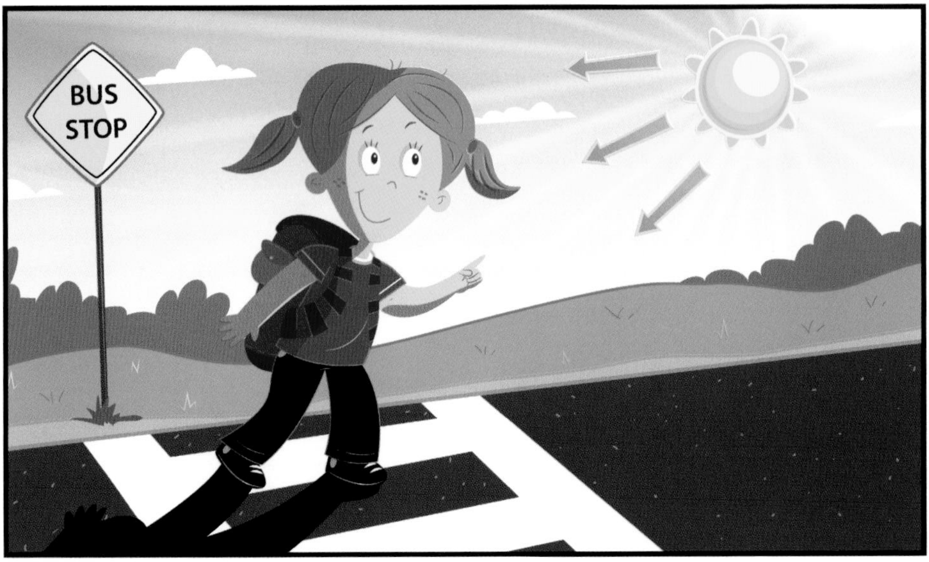
BUS
STOP

Your shadow stretches out.

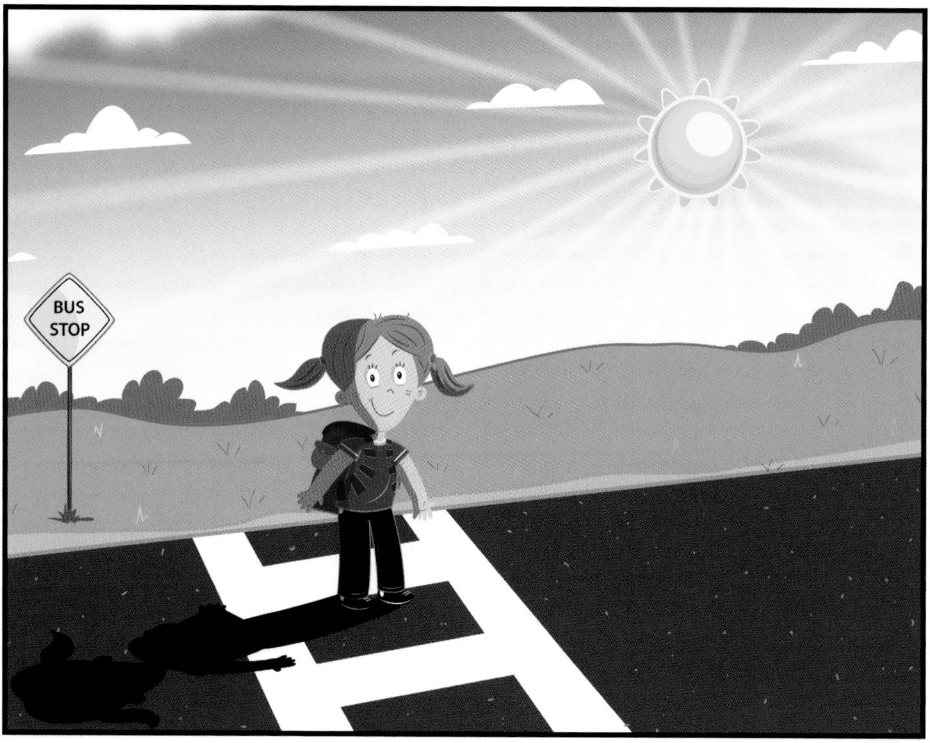
BUS
STOP

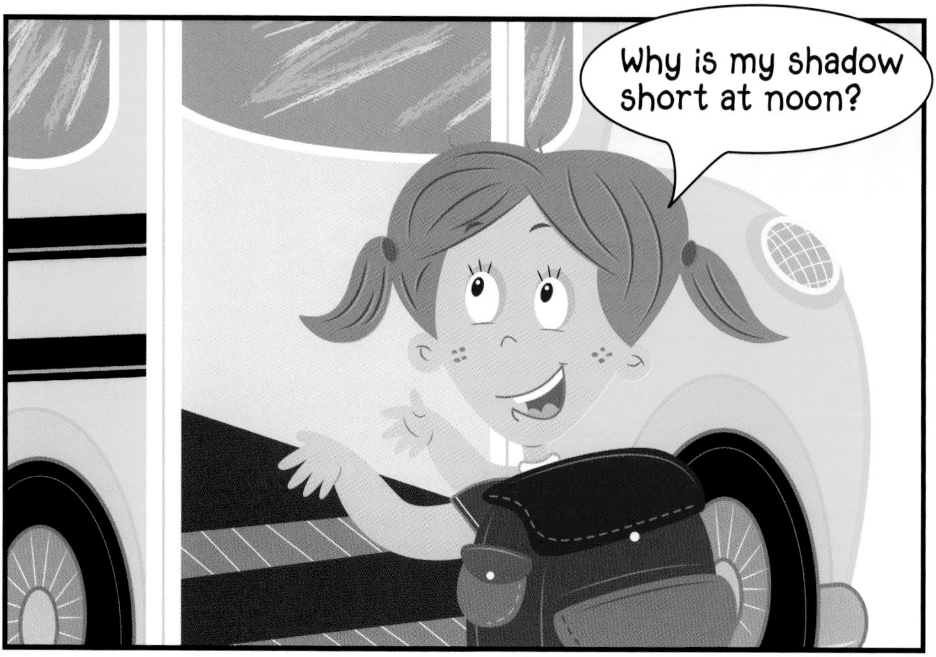
Why is my shadow short at noon?

At noon the sun is closest to being overhead. Sunlight hits you from above.

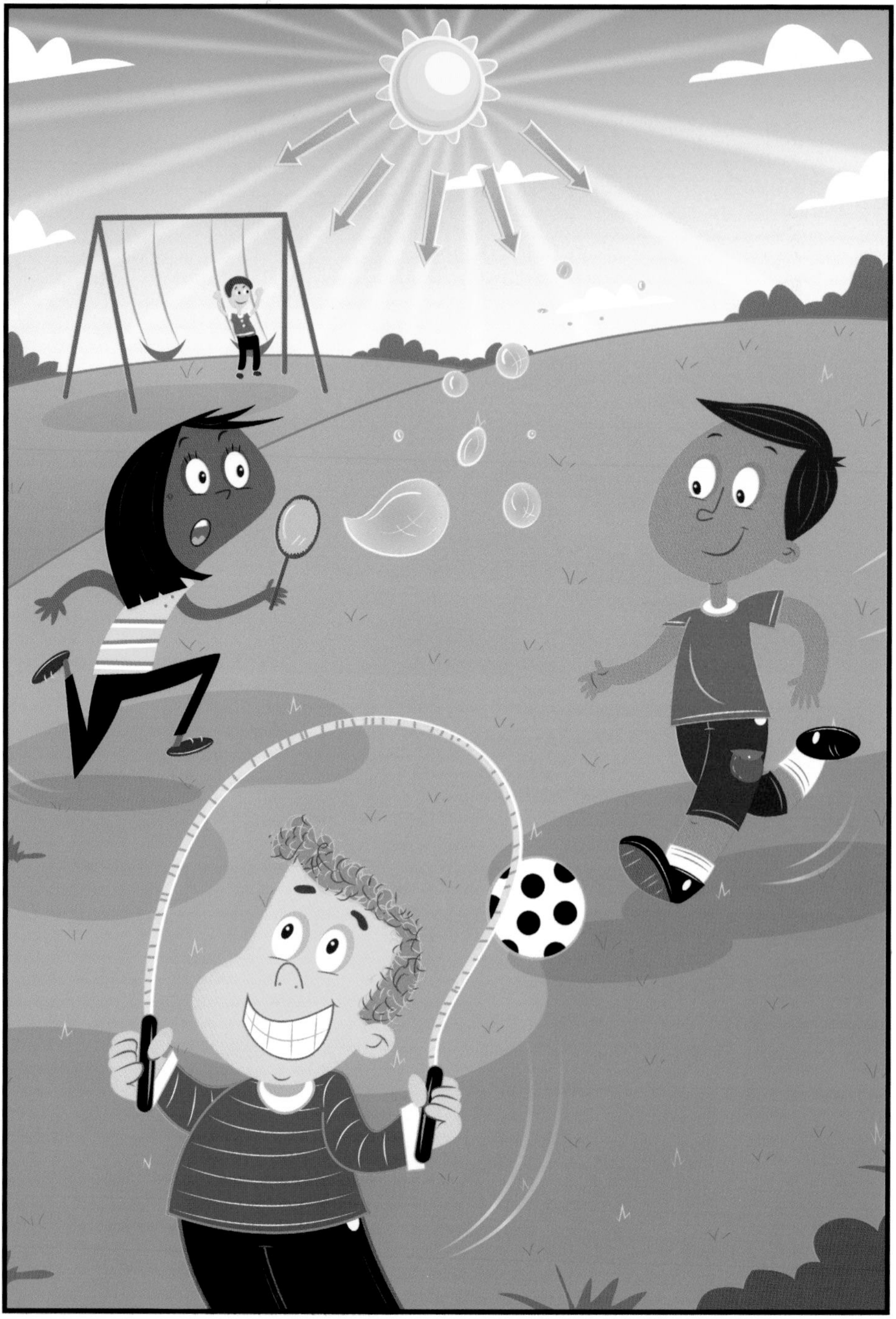

Your shadow looks short.

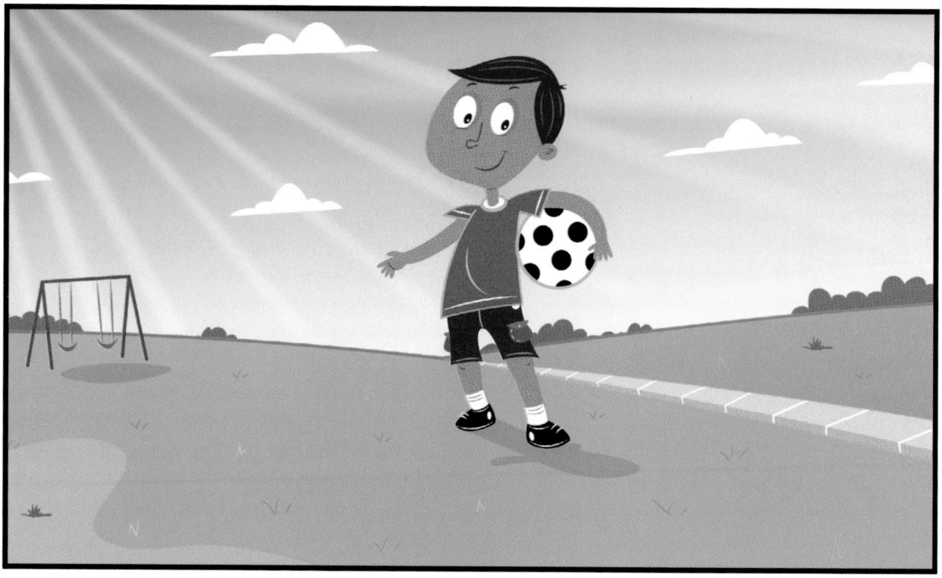

The sun's position doesn't just affect shadows.
It can make days seem longer.

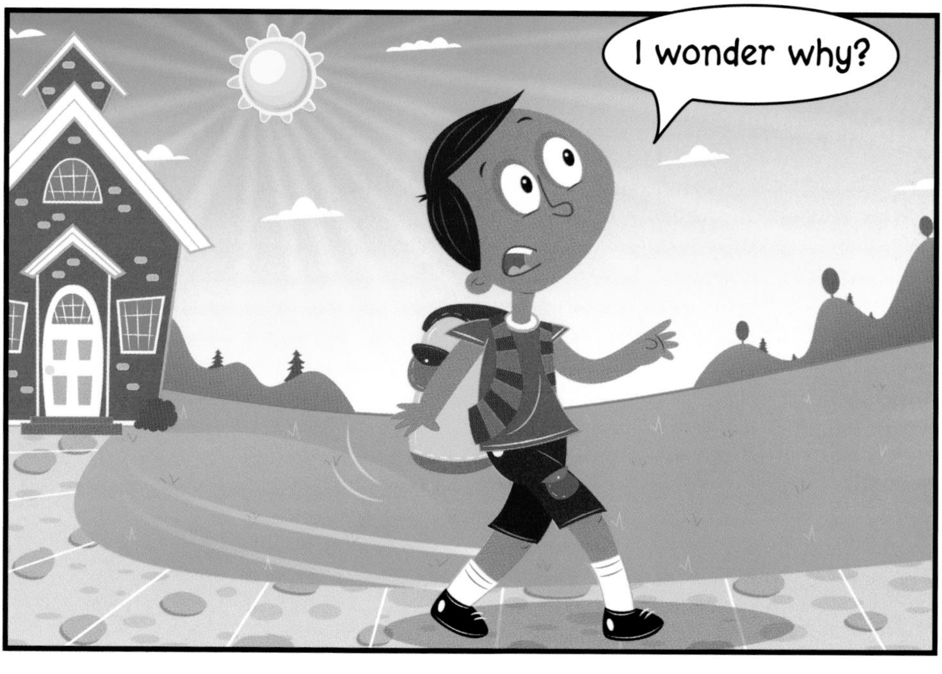
I wonder why?

Why Do the Daylight Hours Change?

Days are always 24 hours long. But the number of daylight hours changes during the year.

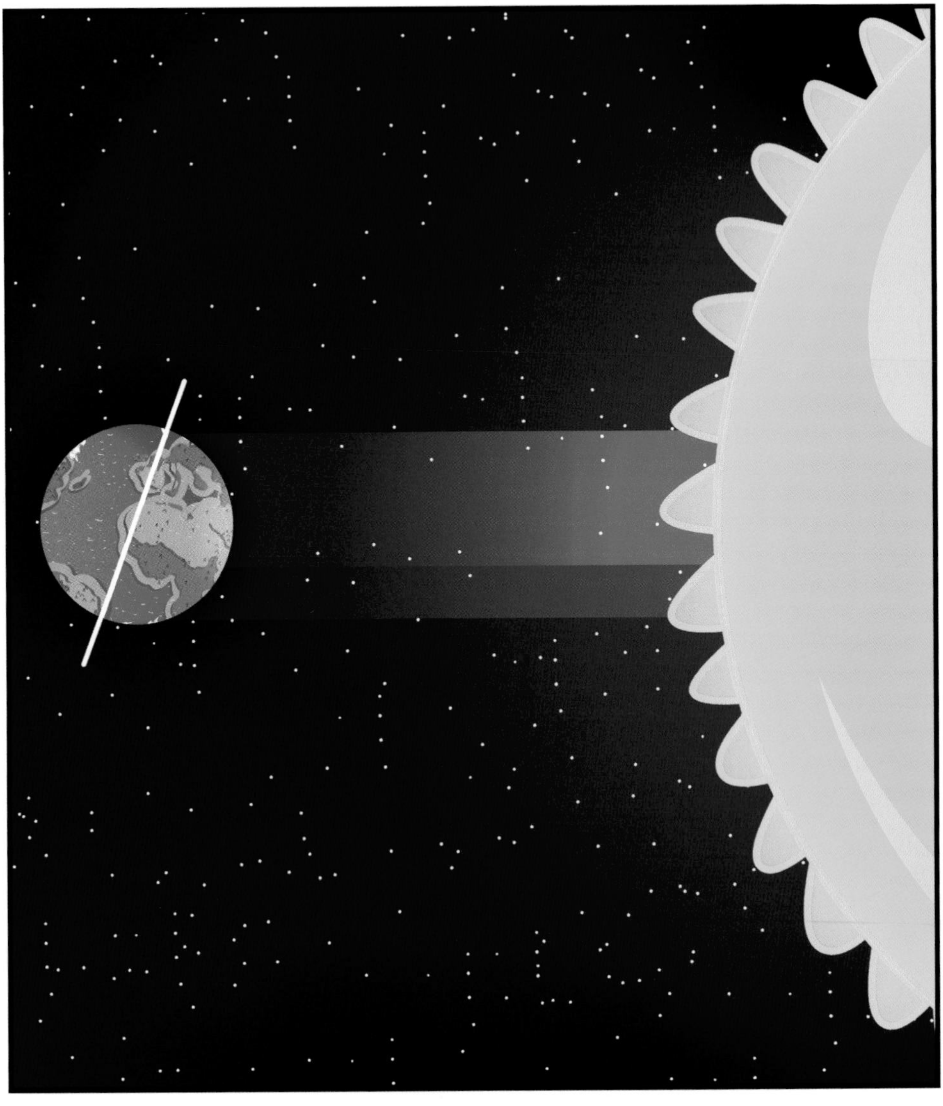

Earth spins on a tilt. In the summer, your part of Earth is tilted toward the sun.

You get more of the sun's light.

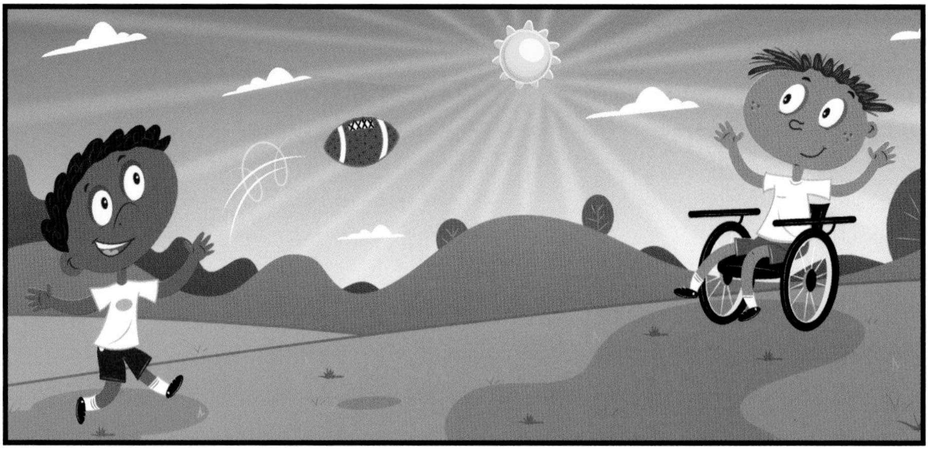

The sun is almost overhead. The days have more daylight hours.

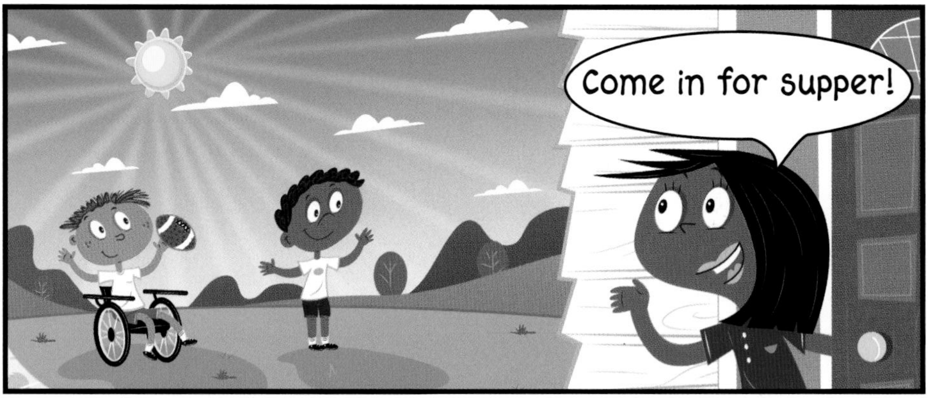
Come in for supper!

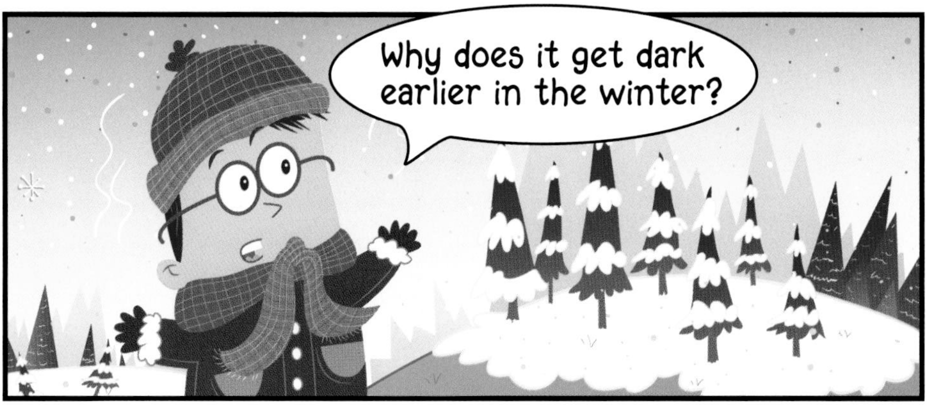
Why does it get dark earlier in the winter?

In the winter, your part of Earth is tilted away from the sun.

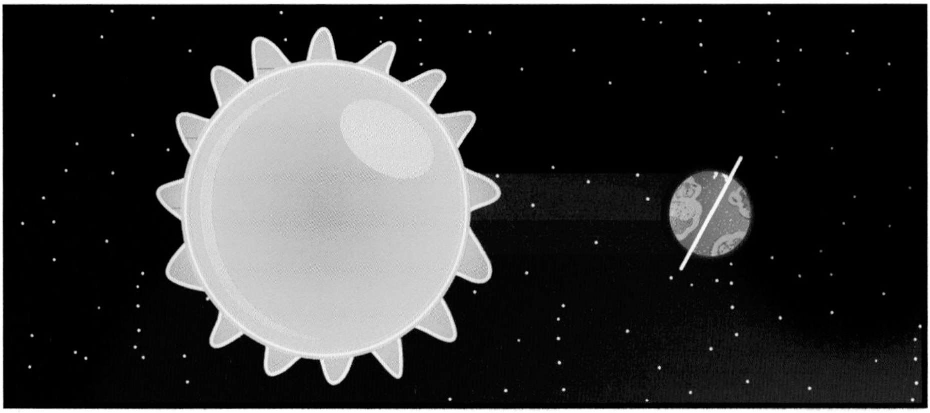

You get less of the sun's light.

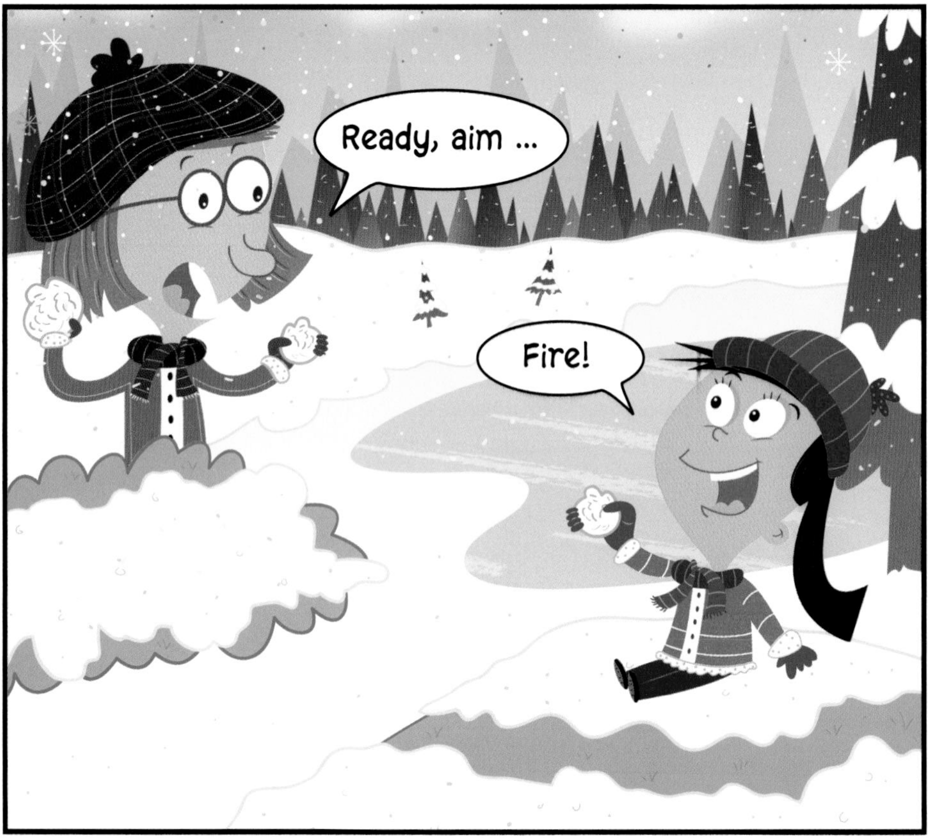
Ready, aim ...
Fire!

The sun never gets very high in the sky.
The days have fewer daylight hours.

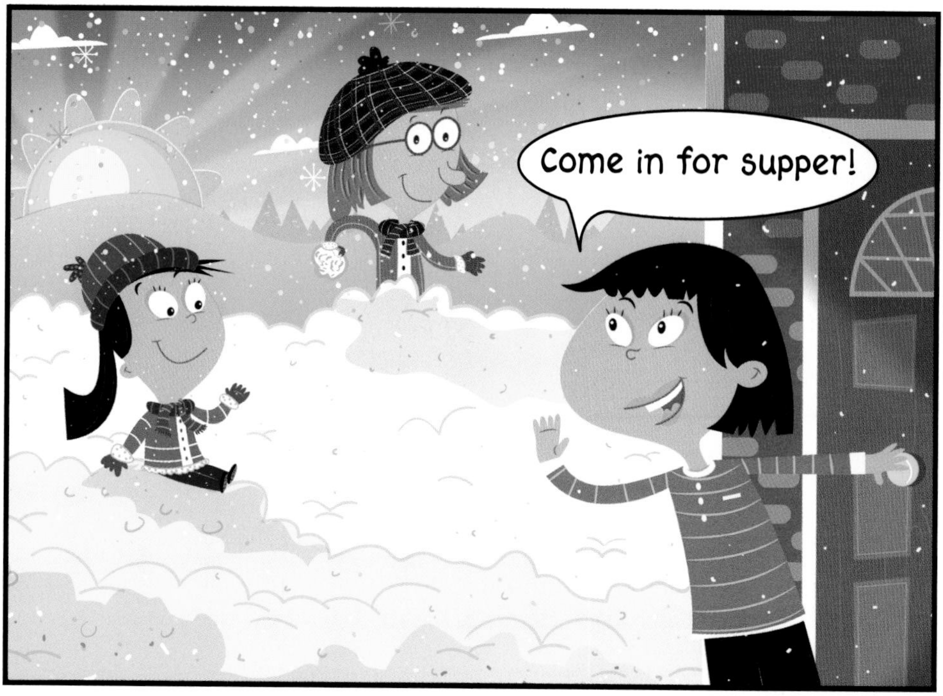
Come in for supper!

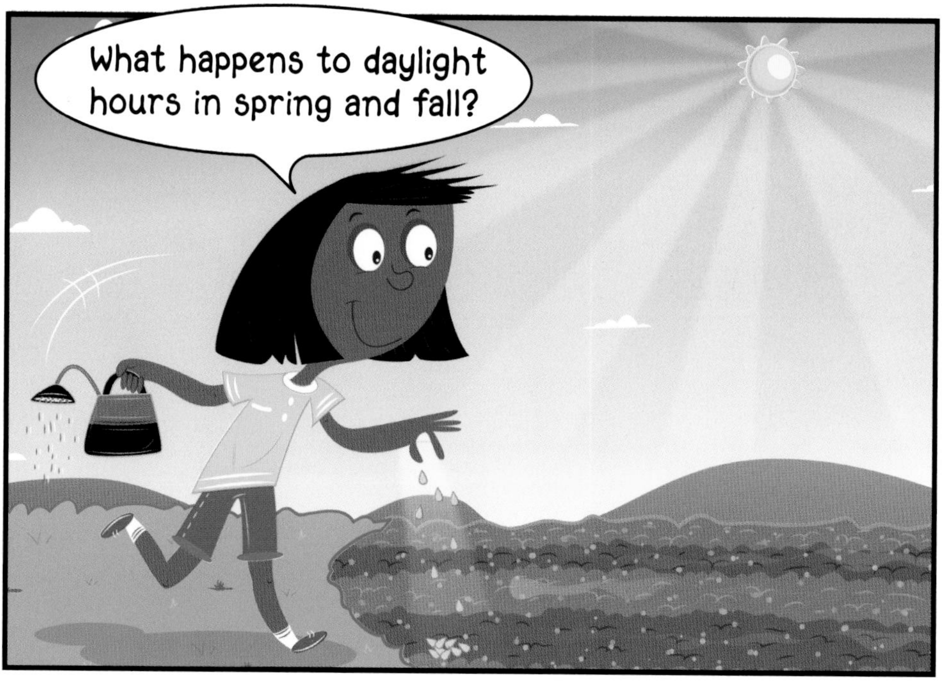
What happens to daylight hours in spring and fall?

Earth's path around the sun makes the seasons change. As winter turns to spring, the daylight hours grow longer.

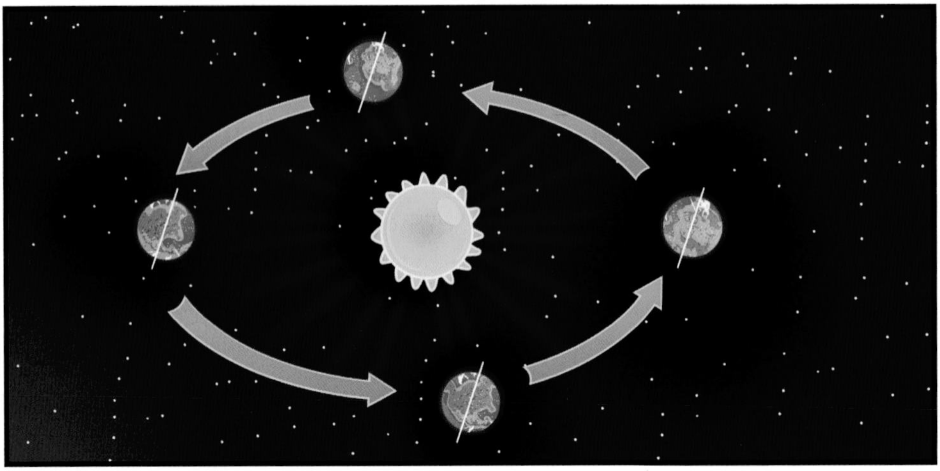

For one day in March, daytime and nighttime are the same length.

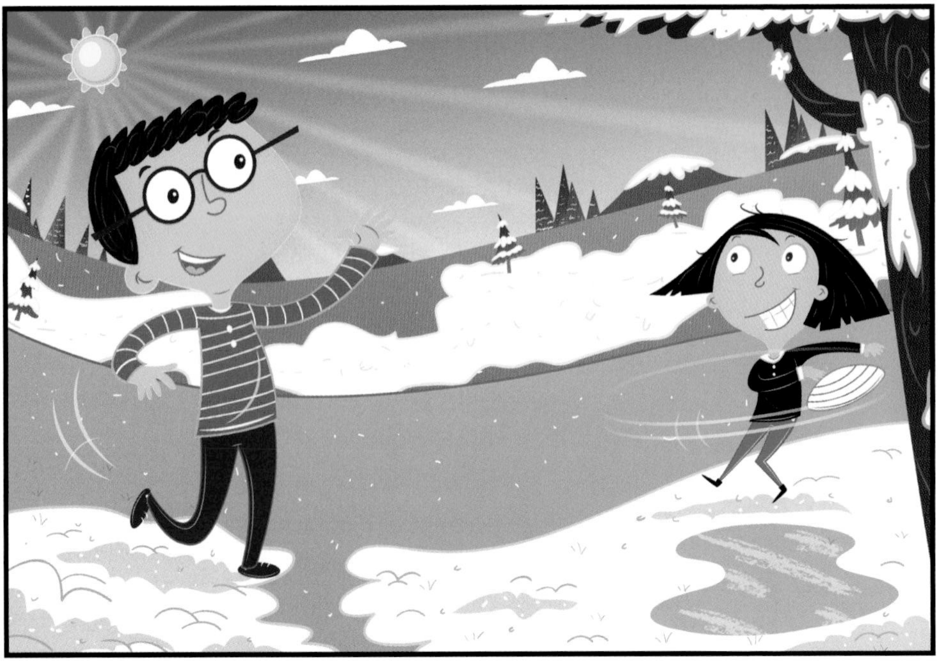

As summer turns to fall, the daylight hours grow shorter. For one day in September, daytime and nighttime are the same length again.

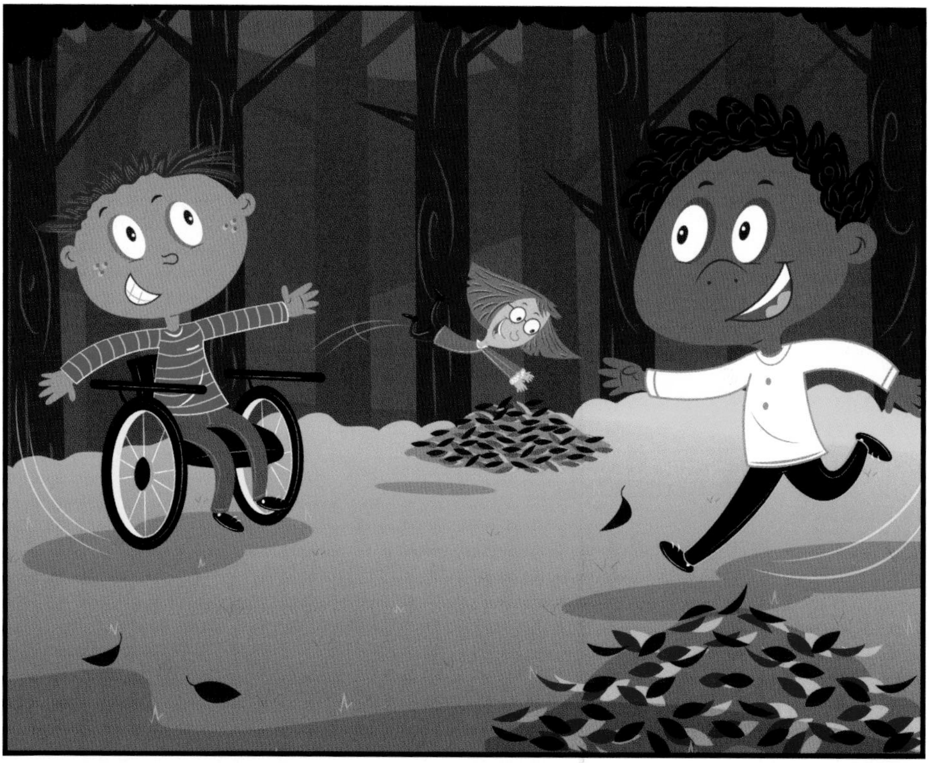

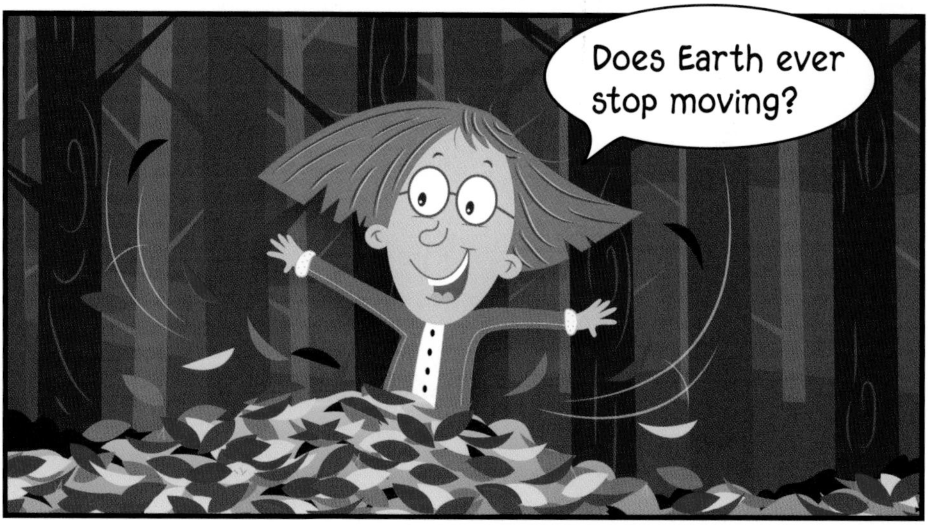
Does Earth ever stop moving?

Earth never stops moving.

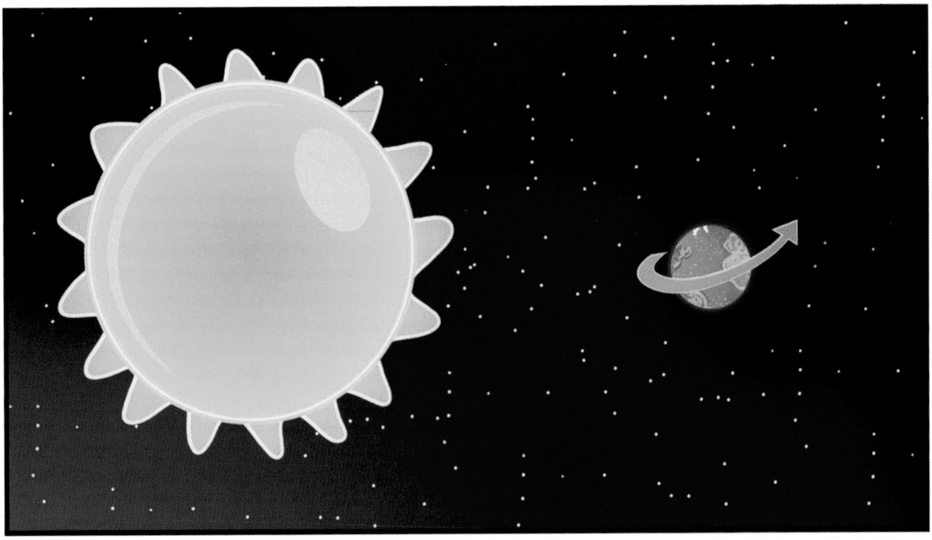

If it stopped spinning, we wouldn't have day and night.

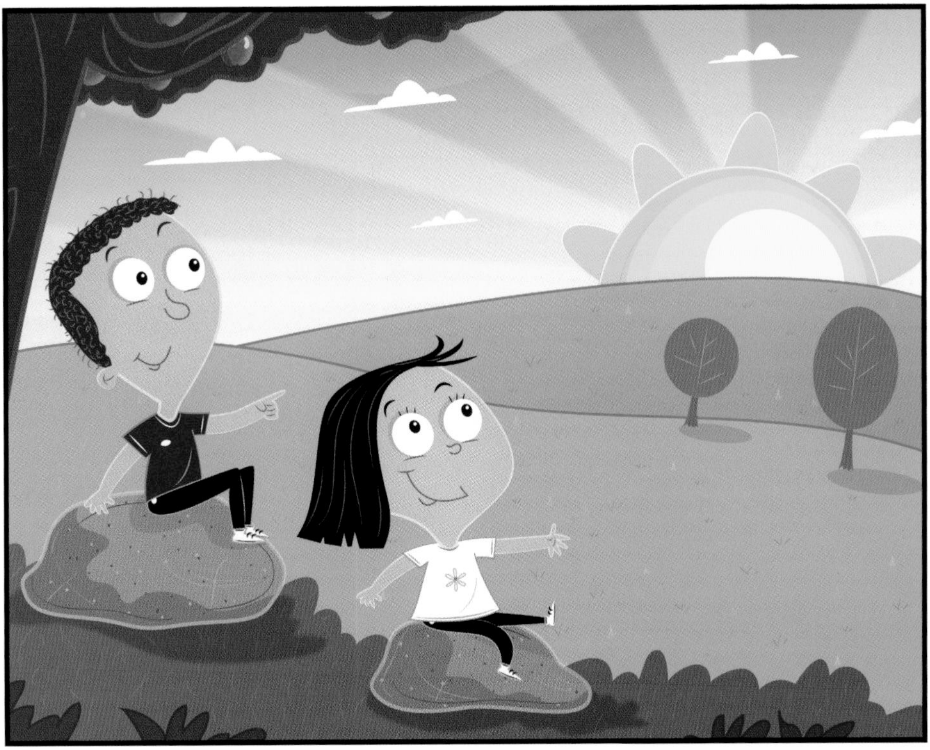

If it stopped circling the sun, the seasons wouldn't change.

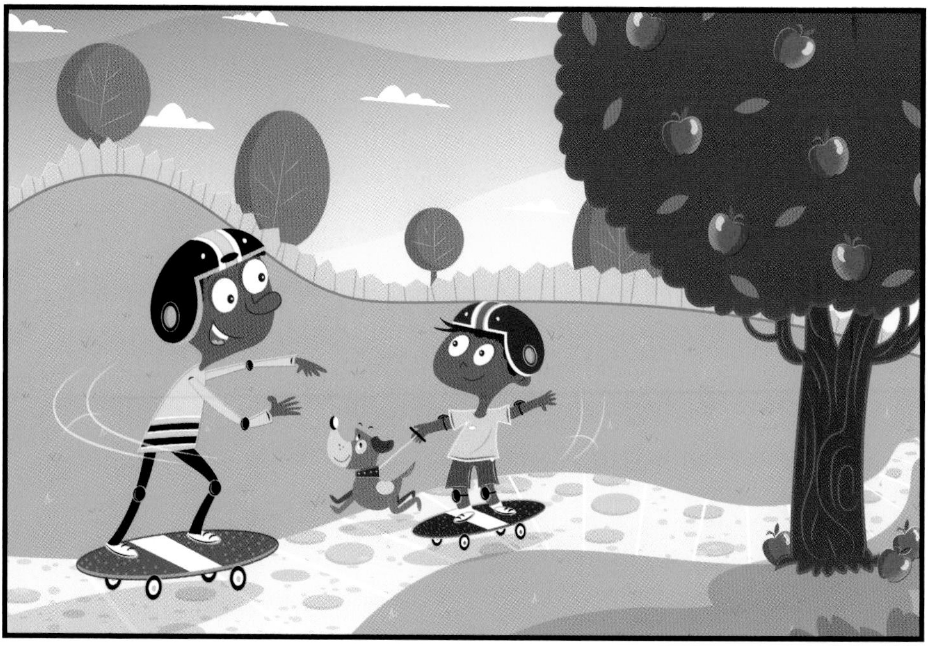

Earth's movement brings each new day and each new season.

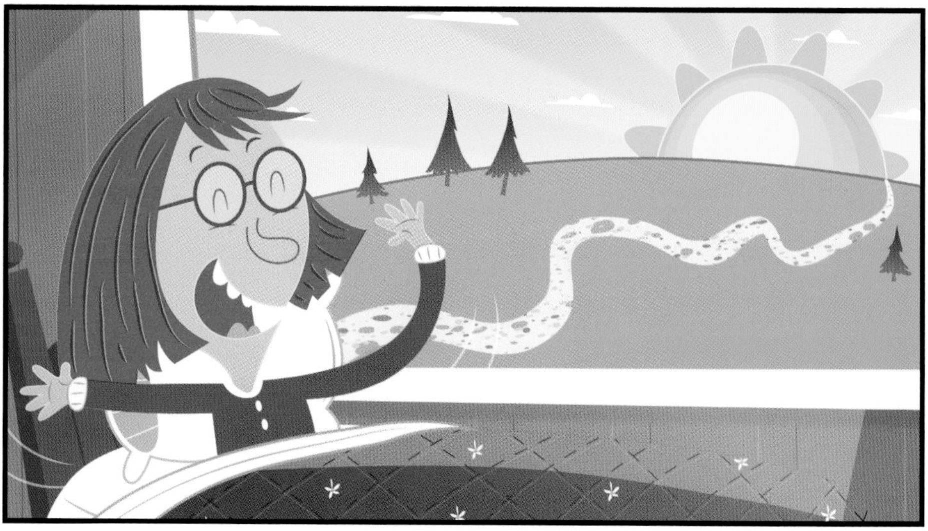

GLOSSARY

dawn—the time when light first appears in the morning

dusk—the time when the sun begins to set in the evening

midnight—12:00 in the middle of the night; one day ends and the next day begins at midnight

noon—12:00 in the middle of the day

season—one of the four parts of the year

shadow—a dark shape made when something blocks light

tilt—to lean to one side

Read More

Monroe, Tilda. *What Do You Know about Light?* 20 Questions. Physical Science. New York: PowerKids Press, 2011.

Rustad, Martha E. H. *The Sun.* Out in Space. Mankato, Minn.: Capstone Press, 2009.

Sterling, Kristin. *It's Sunny Today.* What's the Weather Like? Minneapolis: Lerner Publications, 2010.

Internet Sites

FactHound offers a safe, fun way to find Internet sites related to this book. All of the sites on FactHound have been researched by our staff.

Here's all you do:

Visit *www.facthound.com*

Type in this code: 9781429660983

Check out projects, games and lots more at
www.capstonekids.com

INDEX

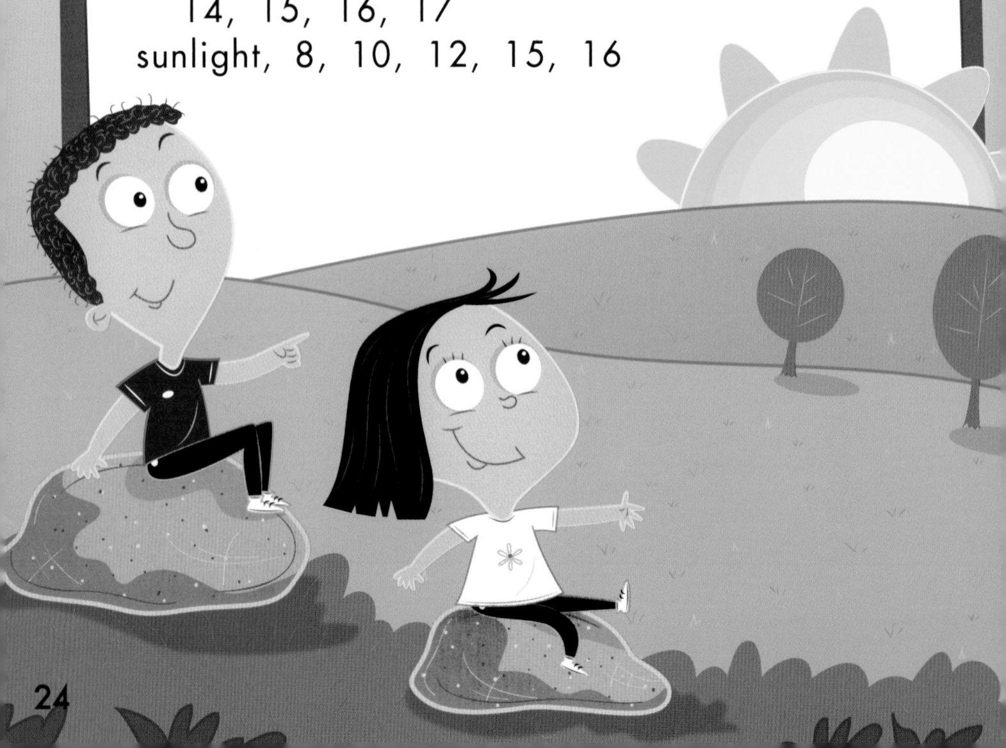

Science Mysteries

Titles in this set:

How do we KNOW about DINOSAURS?
A Fossil Mystery

How DO We STAY on EARTH?
A Gravity Mystery

Where DO the BIRDS GO?
A Migration Mystery

Where DOES the SUN go at NIGHT?
An Earth Science Mystery